Wild Predators!

Wolves and
Other Dogs

Heinemann Library
Chicago, Illinois

Andrew Solway

Design: David Poole and Paul Myerscough
Illustrations: Geoff Ward
Picture Research: Rebecca Sodergren,
Melissa Allison, and Pete Morris

Originated by Ambassador Litho Ltd.
Printed and bound in Hong Kong, China by
South China Printing Co. Ltd.

09 08 07 06 05
10 9 8 7 6 5 4 3 2 1

**Library of Congress Cataloging-in-
Publication Data**
Solway, Andrew.
  Wolves and other dogs / Andrew Solway.
    p. cm. -- (Wild predators)
   ISBN 1-4034-5769-7 (HB library binding) --
ISBN 1-4034-5775-1 (Pbk.)
   1. Wolves--Juvenile literature. 2. Canidae--
Juvenile literature. I. Title. II. Series.
   QL737.C22S66 2004
    599.773--dc22
                                     2004002147

Acknowledgments
The author and publisher are grateful to the
following for permission to reproduce copyright
material:
p. 4 Jeff Lepore/SPL; p. 5 top Laurie
Campbell/Natural History Picture Library; p.5
bottom Tim Davis/SPL; p. 6 Joe
Mcdonald/CORBIS; p. 7 Digital Vision; p. 7 top
Kitchen & V Hurst/NHPA; pp. 8, 12 William
Ervin/SPL; pp. 9, 22, 43 Minden Pictures/Frank
Lane Picture Agency; p. 10 Gerard Lacz/Frank
Lane Picture Agency; p. 11 Mark Newman/Frank
Lane Picture Agency; p. 13 bottom John
Shaw/NHPA; p. 13 top Randy Wells/CORBIS; p.
14 Martin Harvey/NHPA; p. 15 bottom Martin
Harvey/CORBIS; p. 15 top Gallo/CORBIS; p. 16
Peter Pickford/NHPA/; p. 17 bottom Daryl
Balfour/NHPA; p. 17 top Carl and Ann
Purcell/CORBIS; p. 18 Sandford & Agliolo/SPL; p.
19 right Robert Canis/Frank Lane Picture Agency;
p. 19 top Dan Griggs/NHPA; p. 20 Alissa
Crandall/CORBIS; p. 21 right Jason Venus/Natural
Visions; p. 21 top Pat & Tom Leeson/SPL; p. 23
bottom Henry Ausloos/NHPA; p. 23 top D. Robert
& Lori Franz/CORBIS; p. 24 Anthony
Mercieca/SPL; p. 25 Nigel Dennis/SPL; p. 26 Peter
Blackwell/BBC Natural History Unit; p. 27 Fritz
Polking/Frank Lane Picture Agency; pp. 28, 29 S
& D & K Maslowski/Frank Lane Picture Agency; p.
30 Wardene Weisser/Ardea; p. 31 bottom
SAL/Oxford Scientific Films/Rick Price; p. 31 top
Paul A. Souders/CORBIS; p. 32 Haroldo Palo
Jr./NHPA; p. 33 Art Wolfe/SPL; pp. 34, 39 Terry
Whittaker/Frank Lane Picture Agency; p. 35 Nick
Gordon/Oxford Scientific Films; p. 36 FLPA/Jurgen
and Christine Sohns; p. 37 Jean Paul
Ferrero/Ardea; p. 38 K. Ghani/NHPA; pp. 40, 41 J
& A Scott/Natural History Picture Library; p. 42
Gallo Images/CORBIS.

Cover photograph of a North American gray wolf
reproduced with permission of John Shaw/NHPA.
Title page photograph of a white wolf reproduced
with permission of CORBIS.

Every effort has been made to contact copyright
holders of any material reproduced in this book.
Any omissions will be rectified in subsequent
printings if notice is given to the publisher.

The publisher would like to thank Michael Bright,
Senior Producer, BBC Natural History Unit, for his
assistance in the preparation of this book.

Contents

Adaptable Predators

We have very different feelings about domestic (pet) dogs and their wild relations. Dogs live in our homes, and some, such as sheep and cattle dogs, do important jobs for us. But the howling of a wolf sends a shiver down the spine, and most farmers will shoot a fox or a coyote on sight. Dogs, wolves, foxes, and coyotes are all part of the same family called the dogs or canids (family Canidae). Wild or tame, all of them are predators to be reckoned with.

What makes a canid?

Wolves and other canids belong to a larger group of mammals called carnivores (order Carnivora). All carnivores have scissor-like back teeth for slicing through flesh. Most canids are built for long-distance running. They have long legs and a deep chest that gives them stamina (staying power). Canids cannot retract their claws, as cats can. Because they are always scraping on the ground, a canid's claws are blunt. They are used for grip and to hold down prey, rather than as weapons.

Hearing, eyesight, and smell are important senses for canids. Their eyes work well both during the day and at night. African wild dogs that which live on open plains, rely particularly on their eyes for finding prey. Other canids rely more on smell or hearing. Nocturnal hunters, such as foxes, have particularly good hearing, and listen for their prey.

Canids, like this wolf, have large, pointed teeth called canines at the front of the mouth for stabbing into their prey. At the back of the mouth are scissor-like, meat-cutting teeth.

Scavengers

Although they are predators, most canids are very adaptable about what they eat. Foxes, for instance, will live entirely on mice, voles, or rabbits if there is a good supply. But they will also scavenge and eat fruit, insects, worms, or almost any other food. This adaptability helps different kinds of canid to survive in a wide range of habitats, from the Arctic to the Sahara Desert.

Foxes are especially good at adapting to what food is available. In autumn they eat fruit, and they will eat insects and even hunt worms, as this fox is doing.

Domestic dogs and wolves

Pet dogs are direct descendants of wolves that were domesticated by humans about 15,000 years ago. The earliest known fossil of a domestic dog is about 14,000 years old. These early dogs probably looked like dingoes (see page 36). Today there are many different kinds of domestic dogs. People have bred different kinds of dog for different purposes. Long-legged wolfhounds and greyhounds, for instance, were bred as fast-running hunters, while short-legged terriers were bred to go down animal burrows. Beagles, like this one, were bred to hunt by smell. Although there are huge differences between different kinds of dog, all of them belong to the same species: *Canis familaris*.

Gray Wolf

When the pack first attacks, the moose charges at its attackers. But the wolves leap away before it can get near. The moose turns around and charges again, then it panics and begins to run. The wolves follow, leaping at its back and sides. Soon the repeated attacks take their toll, and the moose slows down. The pack leader chooses his moment, then goes for the moose's throat.

Biggest in the family

Gray wolves are the biggest animals in the canid family. A large wolf can be 5 ft (1.5 m) long not counting its tail, 3 ft (1 m) high at the shoulder and weigh 165 lbs (75 kg). Male wolves are bigger than females.

Small populations of gray wolves live in Europe, the Middle East, and the U.S., but most live in northern North America, Russia, and central Asia.

Packing together

Wolves usually live and hunt in packs (groups). These are usually made up of around six or seven wolves, but can be more. At the core of the pack are an adult male and female that have mated and produced young. This pair, called the alpha pair, are the pack leaders. Other wolves in the pack may be family members—offspring of the alpha pair that have grown up. But other wolves from outside the family group may also be accepted into the pack.

Wolves are best known for hunting prey in packs, but they also hunt alone for smaller prey such as lemmings, hares, beavers, and voles.

A new family

The alpha male and female mate in the winter months. The rest of the pack helps to feed and protect the alpha pair's cubs, to give them the best chance of survival. In early spring the alpha pair find or dig a den consisting of a hole or cave. About nine weeks after mating the female gives birth. Usually she will produce five or six cubs.

At first, a wolf cub's eyes are closed, it cannot hear and it is very weak. At first the cubs feed on their mother's milk every two hours, and the female remains with them in the den. After about two weeks the cubs' eyes open, and the female spends less time with them.

Gray wolves are not always gray. Their coat can vary from white to jet-black. Most Arctic wolves, for instance, are white or yellowish.

Wolves around the world

Although gray wolves are all one species there are several types in different parts of the world. Arctic wolves are found in the far north: they are the biggest wolves. Common wolves are medium-sized and live in the forests of Europe and Asia, while timber wolves are medium-sized wolves found in North America. Steppe wolves are small wolves that live in grassland (steppe) in Russia.

A wolf mother with her cubs. The cubs' eyes are blue at first, but they gradually change to the yellow of an adult.

Defending the territory

While the alpha female is with her cubs in the den, the rest of the pack establish a territory around it. This is an area in which the pack can find enough food and water to feed themselves and the new cubs. The pack defends this territory against other wolves. They mark the borders by scent-marking. This means they leave droppings or patches of urine on prominent spots such as trees or large rocks. Other wolves can tell from these scent marks that a pack has claimed the area.

By about two months old the cubs are playing outside the den. At this point they are ready to eat meat. The other pack members begin to help feed the cubs. They catch food and eat it, then come back to the den and regurgitate some for the cubs.

Fall and winter

By fall the cubs are well grown and can travel with the pack, although they are not yet big enough to help in the hunting. At this time of year some of the young wolves that were born the previous year may leave, hoping to find a mate and begin their own pack.

In northern areas, important prey such as caribou travel to their breeding grounds in the fall. Wolf packs in these areas move to follow their prey.

When wolves make a large kill, the alpha wolves get to eat first, followed by wolves in the next rank, and so on.

Musk oxen protect their calves from a wolf pack by forming a defensive ring of adults, with the calves in the middle. The wolves try to break the ring in one place, then dash in and grab a calf.

Hunting in a pack

Wolves live together in packs because by working together they can catch large prey such as moose, elk, deer, goats, bison, and musk oxen. When they hunt alone they usually catch smaller mammals such as lemmings or hares. In winter many small animals hibernate, so wolves can eat better by hunting in a pack. A caribou or moose may take more effort to catch than a lemming, but it will feed the whole pack for several days.

Wolves are clever animals, and they need all of their intelligence for successful hunting. They first find their prey through smell, either by following a scent trail on the ground or by picking up the scent of prey in the air. The wolves move toward this scent, trying to get as close as possible without the prey noticing. Deer and moose can outrun a wolf if they have a reasonable start, but if the wolves can get close before they attack the prey is unlikely to escape.

If the wolves are attacking a herd of animals such as deer, they will look for a straggler outside the main herd. With all large prey they begin by attacking the flanks (sides) and rump (rear) to weaken the animal. Then one wolf, usually the alpha male, will go for the animal's nose or throat.

Keeping in touch

Wolves need to communicate when hunting, and also to avoid conflict within the pack. A wolf's expression and body language say a lot to other wolves. When one wolf is dominant over another, the dominant wolf stands with ears erect and tail high, whereas the lower ranking wolf half-crouches with ears back, tail between its legs, and lips pulled back in a smile-like expression. When a cub begins to get rough, it puts on a playful expression, to show that it is not seriously fighting.

Touch and smell are also important in wolf communication. Scent marks are used to mark territory, and wolves in the same pack greet each other by rubbing their heads together, or by smelling or licking each other. These daily contacts help to strengthen the bonds between pack members.

Wolves keep in touch at a distance by howling. This is particularly important in forests, where it is hard to see far. Wolves also sometimes howl together to show their strength to neighboring packs.

Howling is one way that wolves can communicate over long distances. Each wolf has its own distinctive howl.

Saving wolves

At one time, gray wolves were spread throughout North America, Europe, and Asia. But in some areas humans have wiped out the wolves, and in other areas there are only small populations left. People hunt wolves for sport, while farmers kill wolves because they fear they will eat their livestock. Also, much of the land that wolves once lived on has been cleared for farming or to build towns and cities.

In parts of North America and Europe the wolf is now protected, and in a few of these areas their numbers are gradually increasing. In places such as the U.S. Yellowstone National Park, wolves had been wiped out in the past, but conservation workers have now reintroduced them by bringing in wolves from elsewhere. However, there is still a long way to go before wolves and people can live together in harmony.

In this picture the top wolf is dominant, as shown by its erect ears and high tail. The other wolf is showing submission by lying down, ears back, and tucking its tail between its legs.

Red wolves

In the eastern United States there used to be a species of wolf with a reddish color to its coat, known as the red wolf. Today these red wolves have almost completely died out, with only a few remaining in captivity and around 100 living in the wild. However, new studies suggest that some of the gray wolves in southeastern Canada may in fact be red wolves, or hybrids of red and gray wolves. And some of what scientists think of as coyotes may be hybrids of red wolves and coyotes.

Coyote

The coyote has been following the badger all night. Now the badger has found a rabbit burrow and is digging open the entrance. Soon a rabbit pops out of another hole and begins to run. The coyote begins to chase it, and within a few minutes it is eating supper.

Growing population

Coyotes are smaller and slimmer than wolves. They are 18 to 25 in. (45 to 63 cm) tall at the shoulder, with a narrow muzzle and long, slender legs. Originally coyotes were grassland animals, living in the western United States. But as wolf populations in the U.S. fell, coyotes grew in numbers and moved into new areas. They can now be found in much of North and Central America.

Wily hunters

Coyotes usually hunt at night and they rely upon their keen eyesight, smell, and hearing to follow prey. They mainly eat rodents and rabbits, but they also eat birds, lizards, fruit, and larger prey such as deer. Coyotes also kill farm livestock, especially sheep. For this reason farmers regularly kill them.

Even in the snow, a coyote's super-sensitive nose can follow the scent of a rabbit to its burrow.

Coyotes hunt in different ways. When hunting mice or rats, coyotes stalk their prey until they are close enough to pounce. When hunting fast-moving prey such as a jackrabbit, they chase their victim until it is exhausted. To catch large prey, coyotes usually hunt in packs.

Living in packs

Coyotes mate in the winter, and this is also the time when they most often hunt large prey, so in winter they often live together in packs. As with wolves, an alpha male and female lead the pack, and these are the only pair to breed.

Coyotes are the noisiest of all the canids. They howl to advertise their presence to other coyotes, yelp when playing, and bark as a threat when protecting a den.

A coyote pack defends a territory and marks its boundaries with scent marks. The size of territory a pack needs varies according to how rich the area is in food. It may be over 40 square miles (100 square kilometers), or as small as 1 square mile (3 square kilometers).

Bringing up pups

Female coyotes give birth about nine weeks after mating. Coyote pups are born helpless, but become active soon after their eyes open at about two weeks old. From about three weeks on the male helps to feed the pups. Other pack members guard the pups, but do not help with feeding.

Coyotes sometimes follow American badgers that dig out rodent and rabbit burrows. The coyotes catch any prey that try to escape.

From about eight or ten weeks old, the young coyotes go on hunting trips. In the fall some young coyotes leave the pack, but some may stay on for another year.

Ethiopian Wolf

As the female wolf trots up to the low cliff, three cubs come bounding out of a small cave. The cubs leap at their mother, whining, and licking her muzzle. After a few moments the mother regurgitates some food, and the cubs fall on it eagerly.

Highland wolves

Ethiopian wolves (also known as Simien jackals or Abyssinian wolves) are found only on high moorlands in a few mountainous areas of Ethiopia. They are long-legged but lightly built, with large ears, a narrow muzzle, and small teeth. Their coat is reddish, with white underparts, and they have a white tip to their tail.

The main prey of Ethiopian wolves are giant mole rats and grass rats. Most of the time the wolves hunt alone and when they spot a victim, they sneak up quietly before making a final short dash to grab the prey. Although Ethiopian wolves hunt alone, they live in packs. They do this to protect their rodent-rich territory. Every morning and evening the wolves patrol the borders of their territory, leaving scent marks as a sign of ownership. Sometimes there are disputes between neighboring packs during these patrols. These involve lots of growling and barking, but there is rarely a fight.

Ethiopian wolves look more like tall foxes than wolves. However, modern studies suggest that they are closely related to gray wolves and coyotes.

Ethiopian wolves usually hunt alone, as here. But sometimes small groups of wolves will hunt together to catch larger prey such as hares or young nyala (antelopes).

Mating and cubs

Unlike gray wolf packs, Ethiopian wolf packs do not have a mating pair at their center. The reason for this is that all the members of the pack are close relatives, and if they mated it would lead to inbreeding. Instead, the dominant female in each pack almost always mates with a male from a neighboring pack.

As with wolves and coyotes, the female gives birth in a den. The pups feed on her milk for the first four weeks, then they begin to eat regurgitated food. Other pack members then help to feed the pups. The pups continue to be fed by the pack until they are six months old.

Close to extinction

Ethiopian wolves are found in only a few small areas, and even in the largest of these there are just a few hundred wolves. The species is in great danger of becoming extinct. Conservationists are striving to prevent Ethiopian wolves from dying out completely. Keeping what is left of the wolves' natural habitat is important, as is preventing domestic dogs from breeding with the wolves and hunting their prey. These wolves eat one species of African mole rat and mountain nyalas, such as this one, also found only in the Ethiopian highlands.

15

Jackals

Ears pricked, the jackal turns slowly toward the tiny noise in the grass. There is little to be seen in the darkness, but the jackal does not need to see. It leaps high into the air and pounces, forefeet first. There is a short squeak, then silence as the jackal kills the rat with a bite.

Meat and vegetables

Jackals are omnivores: they eat both meat and plant food. Insects, eggs, fruit, vegetables, and even grass are all on a jackal's menu. Jackals are also scavengers, often gathering in groups to pick at the remains of an animal killed by lions or other large predators.

Jackals hunt at night. They most often eat small animals such as rodents, birds, and lizards, or hunt in pairs to catch larger prey such as rabbits, hares, and antelope or gazelle fawns. Jackals will use all kinds of tricks to get food. They have been known to run in among a herd of antelope, distracting them and allowing a cheetah to get in close for the kill. The jackal then gets to eat the cheetah's leftovers.

Jackals will hang around the kill of large predators, hoping to get the leftovers. However, only about one-tenth of what they eat is carrion.

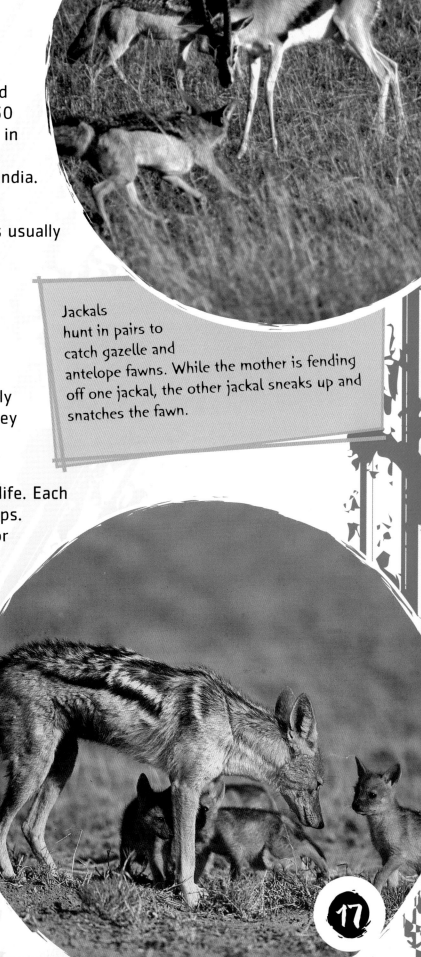

Three types

There are three different species of jackal: golden, side-striped, and black-backed jackals. They are all medium-sized canids, between 12 and 20 in. (30 and 50 cm) tall at the shoulder. They live mainly in Africa, but the golden jackal also lives in southeast Europe, the Middle East, and India.

The three different kinds of jackal live in different types of habitat. Golden jackals usually live in dry areas, although not usually in deserts. Black-backed jackals live in grasslands and other open areas, while side-striped jackals prefer woodlands.

Family groups

Jackals usually live in pairs or small family groups rather than in packs, although they gather in large numbers when there is a good source of food.

Male and female jackals usually pair for life. Each year they find a den to bring up their pups. Often they use an old aardvark burrow or termite mound. About nine weeks after mating the female gives birth. There are usually between two and nine pups. By three months old the pups go on hunting trips with their parents. Some young jackals leave once they have developed their hunting skills, but others stay with the family and become helpers for next year's litter.

Jackals hunt in pairs to catch gazelle and antelope fawns. While the mother is fending off one jackal, the other jackal sneaks up and snatches the fawn.

Jackal pups, such as these side-stripes, start eating regurgitated food when 2 weeks old, but they still need some milk until about 10 weeks of age.

17

Red Fox

It is 3 A.M. in Bristol, United Kingdom, and a fox is on a regular patrol through its territory. Near a dumpster at the back of a bakery it catches a rat. In a garbage can outside the restaurant it finds a half-eaten pizza. Then the fox trots off to a nearby garden to raid the bird feeder.

A great success

Red foxes are clever and resourceful animals that can find food almost anywhere. They are among the most widespread of all land mammals. They live in Europe, Asia, north Africa, North America, and Australia. They can survive in all kinds of habitats, from Arctic tundra to city centers.

Red foxes have been introduced into some areas by humans. European foxes were introduced into North America in the 17th century (although there were already some red foxes in the northeast of the continent). In the 19th century red foxes were also introduced into Australia.

Cat-like dogs

In many ways foxes are more cat-like than wolves and other canids (those in the genus Canis). For a start, red foxes are smaller. They are between 14 and 16 in. (35 and 40 cm) tall at the shoulder. Their lighter build allows them to be quicker and more agile. The pupils of their eyes are vertical ovals or slits, similar to a cat's. This gives them better night vision. Also, a fox's whiskers are like a cats in that they are much longer than other dogs.

A red fox's large ears are good for pinpointing sounds, its cat-like eyes have good night vision, and its dagger-like canine teeth can stab deep into its prey.

Most red foxes have reddish fur, but a small percentage have silver fur (black with longer, silvery hairs), or cross fur (a black stripe along the back and another across the shoulders).

Foxy words

A male fox is sometimes called a reynard. Female foxes are vixens and baby foxes are called kits. A group of foxes is called a skulk or a leash.

Hunting for prey

Foxes are best at hunting small mammals such as mice and voles, but will also hunt larger prey such as rabbits. When a fox hunts small prey it moves carefully and quietly, listening for the faintest sounds. Once it hears its prey, the fox moves its head and ears to pinpoint exactly where the animal is. Then it launches itself into a high leap, coming down almost vertically on its prey with its front feet.

Foxes use a high leap similar to a mouse when catching small animals. As youngsters they practice this kind of leaping in play.

Earthworms, fruit, and garbage can scraps

A red fox's diet is not limited to small mammals. Foxes also eat prey as small as insects and worms and, in the fall, large amounts of fruit. They also eat carrion, scavenge scraps from bird feeders, and search through garbage cans for food.

At times when food is plentiful, a red fox caches (hides) extra food. The fox digs shallow holes and buries some food in them. A small amount of food is put into each cache, to avoid losing the whole food store if a hiding place is discovered. Red foxes have extremely good memories for where they have buried food.

Social life

Foxes are solitary hunters, but they usually live in small groups of one male and one or more females. Each group has its own territory, where it can find enough food all year. The foxes regularly leave scent marks around the territory, and any intruder is driven out by force.

The dominant female in a group pairs with the male fox. The pair mate in late winter or early spring and usually three to six kits are born between February and May.

Bringing up young

As with other canids, fox kits are helpless at first and stay in the den with their mother. When they start to eat meat, their father and other females help to feed them. Kits first venture out of the den at about four weeks old. At first they stay close to the entrance, but gradually they become bolder.

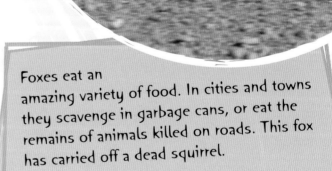

Foxes eat an amazing variety of food. In cities and towns they scavenge in garbage cans, or eat the remains of animals killed on roads. This fox has carried off a dead squirrel.

Fox kits in their den. Female foxes usually prepare more than one den and, if any danger threatens, they move the kits to a different den.

Leaving home

The kits romp around, fighting with each other, chasing insects, and pouncing on sticks. By six months of age they can look after themselves. The males usually leave the family group at this point, and may travel long distances to find a territory. Females tend to stay longer, and travel less distance from their birthplace.

Foxes and rabies

Foxes often suffer from the serious disease, rabies. They can spread this to dogs and sometimes even people. For many years people have tried to control rabies by killing foxes, but with limited success.

Since the 1980s, pieces of meat containing antirabies vaccine have been used to immunize foxes against the disease. This approach has had great success, and large parts of Europe are now free of rabies.

Millions of foxes are killed as pests each year and many more die on the roads or on railway lines. Foxes are also killed for their fur, and for sport.

21

Arctic Fox

The Arctic fox is following a polar bear's trail. Suddenly it becomes more alert as it sees a darker patch on the snow not far ahead. The fox begins to move more cautiously. It does not want to become bear food. But the polar bear has gone, leaving behind a seal carcass with plenty of meat scraps on it.

Northern home

The flat, boggy tundra of the far north is the natural home of the Arctic fox. It lives in northern North America, Asia, and Europe, and on islands such as Greenland and Iceland. Arctic foxes are quite small, about the size of a large cat. They are between 30 and 46 in. (76 and 116 cm) in length; about one-third of this is the fox's long, bushy tail.

In winter the Arctic fox has a thick, white, furry coat. It even has fur on the bottoms of its feet. In spring the Arctic foxes shed this coat for a cooler, gray-brown summer one. A few Arctic foxes have different colored fur: these blue foxes are bluish-gray in winter and chocolate-brown in summer.

A wide range of foods

The most important prey for Arctic foxes are lemmings and other rodents, especially in the summer. They also eat birds and their eggs, fish, berries, carrion, and even grass and seaweed. Arctic foxes can sniff out young seal pups under the snow. They often hide or cache their food as red foxes do.

In the winter Arctic foxes often follow polar bears and scavenge their kill.

Mating and young

Before the end of the Arctic winter, male and female Arctic foxes look for partners and mate. After mating, the pair prepare a den for the kits. The female gives birth seven or eight weeks after mating. Arctic foxes have bigger litters than any other canids. They average five to ten kits, but sometimes have as many as nineteen. The kits are helpless at first, and stay in the den for the first three weeks. By the age of seven or eight weeks they go on hunting trips, and some may leave home. Other kits do not leave until the following spring.

A blue Arctic fox in its winter coat. The Arctic fox's coat is a better insulator than that of any other mammal.

Arctic fox kits near their den. Good den sites are used again and again. Some sites have been in use for hundreds of years.

Lots of lemmings

Feeding a large family of kits is hard work, and the male has to do much of the hunting. At first, a family of 10 or 11 kits needs 30 lemmings or equivalent food each day. This goes up to about 100 lemmings a day just before the young foxes leave home. Altogether it takes 3,500 to 4,000 lemmings to raise an Arctic fox family.

Fennec Fox

A fennec fox is hunting in the Sahara Desert. Its ears prick forward as it picks up the tiny sounds of a snake slithering over the sand. The desert viper is small, but its bite is deadly. The fox runs around the snake, biting at its head again and again. With a final bite the fox crushes the snake's skull, and carries it off to eat underground.

Smallest fox

The fennec fox is the smallest of all the canids. It is smaller than a rabbit, with a head and body length between 9 and 16 in. (24 and 41 cm). Fennec foxes live in the deserts of North Africa and in parts of the Middle East. They are adapted in many ways to survive the harsh desert environment.

Adapted for heat

Most canids pant to lose heat when they are hot. Saliva (spit) on the tongue evaporates and cools the animal down. However, a fennec fox cannot afford to lose precious liquid in this way. Instead, it loses heat through its huge ears. Blood passing through the ears loses heat into the air to help cool the fox down.

A fennec fox has a thick undercoat of fur that keeps out the heat in the day and the cold at night.

Fennec foxes sometimes kill and eat venomous snakes such as vipers. A fennec is not immune to snakebite, but it can eat a dead snake because the venom is made harmless in its stomach.

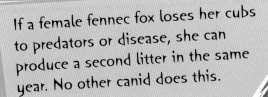

If a female fennec fox loses her cubs to predators or disease, she can produce a second litter in the same year. No other canid does this.

Fur on the soles of its feet stops them from being burned on the hot sand. Studies suggest that fennec foxes do not need to drink at all. They get enough moisture to survive from their food.

Desert living

Fennec foxes spend the day resting in underground dens, and only become active in the cool of the evening. Because of the need to escape the desert heat, they use dens year-round, unlike most other canids.

Fennec foxes live in extended family groups of one male and up to nine vixens. The male and the dominant vixen mate early in the year, and two to five kits are born just over seven weeks later. The kits are gray, rather than the sandy color of the adults.

Night hunting

A fennec fox's ears give it superb hearing as well as helping it cool down. It can pick up the tiniest movements of prey in the darkness. Fennec foxes usually hunt rodents, such as gerbils. But they also eat a wide range of other food, including, rabbits, birds, snakes, lizards, insects, eggs, roots, and fruit such as dates.

Bat-Eared Fox

On the Serengeti plains in Africa, a martial eagle swoops down toward a bat-eared fox in a tremendous dive. The fox hears the eagle coming and begins to run. It runs fast, but not fast enough as the eagle overtakes it. At the last moment, the fox does an almost complete about-face, still running at full speed. The eagle misses its mark, and before it can recover the fox has escaped into its burrow.

Masked foxes

Bat-eared foxes are small, very agile, short-legged foxes with huge ears. The head and body are 18 to 26 in. (46 to 66 cm) long, while the tail is about half this length. Bat-eared foxes live in dry grassland areas in southern and eastern Africa. They have a black mask across their eyes like a raccoon.

Bat-eared foxes have different teeth from other canids. They have at least four extra molars (chewing teeth), a pair in the upper jaw, and a pair in the lower. These extra teeth grind up the tough outer skeletons of insects they eat.

Insect eaters

The main foods of bat-eared foxes are harvester termites and dung beetles. Both these insects are common where there are herds of grazing animals such as zebra and wildebeest. Harvester termites collect the grass that grazing animals eat for their underground nests.

Bat-eared foxes live close to grazing animals, because this is where they find their favorite insect foods. They also sometimes eat fruit, scorpions, and small mammals such as mice. This fox lives in the Masai Mara Game Reserve in Kenya.

Dung beetles feed on the droppings of grazing animals and lay their eggs in balls of dung so the larvae have food to eat when they hatch.

Because their favorite insects are common where there are herds of large grazers, bat-eared foxes live close to these grazers too. In some areas bat-eared foxes hunt for food at night, but in southern Africa they are active during the day in winter. A bat-eared fox's hearing is so good that it can hear the sounds of beetle larvae inside balls of dung.

Family life

Bat-eared foxes live in small family groups. In areas where there is a good supply of food, these groups may live quite close to each other. Fox pairs live in burrows that they dig or take over from other animals. They may have several burrows in their home range, each one with several tunnels and entrances.

About ten weeks after a pair mate, the vixen gives birth to her kits. There are usually between one and six kits in the litter. The young foxes are fully grown at six to nine months old, and usually leave the family group at this age.

Bat-eared fox kits feed on their mother's milk until they are fifteen weeks old. After this they begin to hunt for insects and other food.

27

Gray Fox

A finch is settling on its nest for the night, high in the branches of a tree. But something disturbs it: there is a predator nearby. Calling in alarm, the finch flies off. A few seconds later a gray fox reaches the nest and makes a meal of the finch's eggs.

Woodland foxes

Gray foxes are found from southern Canada to the northern part of South America. They are similar in size to red foxes, measuring 34 to 49 in. (86 to 124 cm) from head to tail, about one-third of which is tail.

Gray foxes live mainly in woodland areas and hunt mostly at night, but they are sometimes active during the daytime. However, like other foxes they are adaptable, and are found in a wide range of habitats, except places that are completely treeless, including urban areas. Unlike other foxes, gray foxes are excellent tree-climbers. They have strong, hooked claws on their hind (back) feet that allow them to scramble up trees.

Varied diets

Like most other foxes, gray foxes have a varied diet. Their main prey are rabbits, mice, rats, and voles. However, they also eat large numbers of insects and, in late summer and fall, fruit is their main food. Birds and climbing animals, such as squirrels are also among the prey they creep up on.

Although gray foxes have a grizzled gray back, they have yellowish fur on their sides, reddish legs, some white on their chest, and a black tip to their tail!

Island gray foxes

About 10,000 years ago, a few gray foxes found their way to the Channel Islands off the coast of California. Scientists think they may have floated there on logs. Isolated from the mainland foxes, they gradually adapted to island life. The main difference from the mainland was that there were few larger prey, so the island foxes ate mostly insects.

Today, island gray foxes, such as this one, are a separate species from those on the mainland. They are smaller and have shorter tails. Island foxes are heavily protected. Dogs, which could cause disease in the foxes, and cats, which could compete with foxes for food, are kept off the six islands where they live.

A den up a tree

Gray foxes use a wide range of different sites for their dens. They may use ground dens such as burrows, hollow logs, or thick bushes. Other times dens are in hollow trees or even old squirrel or hawk nests.

Gray foxes mate in early spring, and kits are born seven or eight weeks later. There are usually three to five kits to a litter and they are born helpless and with eyes closed. Their eyes open after nine to twelve days, and by three months old they are going on hunting trips. In the late summer or fall the family breaks up.

Zorros

On the dry pampas of Argentina a young lamb has lost its mother. Although it bleats pitifully, the other sheep take little notice. But another animal is very interested in the lamb. A culpeo fox, hidden by a dip in the ground, creeps slowly closer to the bleating lamb . . .

Wolf-like foxes

Culpeos are one of several kinds of fox found in South America. These South American foxes are known as zorros (*zorro* is the Spanish word for fox). They are stockier and more wolf-like in appearance than other foxes. In fact, one 19th-century scientist called them "fox-tailed wolves."

Zorros are found in a wide range of different habitats, from deserts to rain forests. Culpeos are found in the foothills of the Andes and on the pampas of Argentina. Farmers often kill them because they hunt lambs.

Crab-eating zorros

Crab-eating zorros are found in much of northern and eastern South America. They live mainly in savanna grasslands, woodlands, and plains. They are medium-sized foxes, about 3 ft (1 m) long, one-third of which is tail. Crab-eating zorros are gray-brown, with reddish legs and face, and white underparts.

Although they are called crab-eating zorros, the land crabs that they eat are only a small part of their diet. Like most foxes they will hunt small rodents, but they also eat frogs and lizards, turtles' eggs, vegetables, and fruit such as bananas.

Crab-eating zorros are probably the most widespread of the ten species of South American fox.

Culpeos are the largest zorros, 63 in. (160 cm) from head to tail.

Crab-eating zorros live most often in pairs. The pairs mate in December, and the young are born seven to eight weeks later. Crab-eating zorros usually use the old burrows of other animals as dens, rather than digging their own.

Three to six kits are usually born. They need their mother's milk until they are three months old, but by the time they reach eight months they are considered adults.

Other zorros

Gray zorros, like this one, are one of the smallest zorros. Sometimes they are only 28 in. (72 cm) from head to tail. Gray zorros have been heavily hunted for their pale gray fur. In the early 1980s, nearly half a million gray zorros were killed for the fur trade, but in recent years fewer foxes have been hunted. One zorro that little is known about is the small-eared zorro. It is one of the few foxes that lives in the rain forests.

Maned Wolf

A maned wolf is out looking for food. It finds a twisted, thorny bush with large hairy leaves. The bush has fruit on it that looks like yellow tomatoes. The maned wolf sniffs at the fruit and then begins to eat hungrily. This is *fruta de lobo* (wolf's fruit), and it helps kill worm parasites that can grow in the wolf's gut.

A fox on stilts

The maned wolf is the biggest canid in South America. Although it is called a wolf, it is not a close relative of the true wolves. It looks more like a tall fox (it has been described as a "red fox on stilts"), but it is not a true fox either. It does not have a fox's cat-like eyes, for instance.

The maned wolf is found in grasslands and river areas in eastern South America. Its coat is mainly red, but it has what looks like black socks and a short black mane running down its neck and shoulders. Its long legs make it very tall: it can stand 31 in. (79 cm) at the shoulder.

Feeding

Like foxes, maned wolves are omnivores. About half of a maned wolf's diet is wolf's fruit. The maned wolf also hunts prey as big as pacas (large rodents) that can weigh 18 lbs (8 kg). However, it more often catches smaller rodents, rabbits, armadillos, birds, and sometimes chickens. When catching small prey, the maned wolf pounces on them like a fox.

Maned wolves often live near rivers or in boggy areas. Their feet can splay (spread) as they walk. This stops them from sinking into wet grassland.

32

Night hunters

Maned wolves are usually nocturnal, although they also hunt in the early morning and late evening. Because of their long legs they are not good burrowers, and their dens are aboveground, in thick bushes, or in crevices between rocks.

Social life

Maned wolves usually live in pairs in large territories that they will scent-mark and defend against outsiders. Within these territories the wolves are solitary, hunting and sleeping alone except during the breeding season.

A female maned wolf gives birth to cubs about 65 days after mating. The newborn cubs are blind and helpless, but they develop quickly. After 9 days their eyes and ears are open, and at 4 weeks they begin to take solid food. As among wolves and wild dogs, the adults feed the cubs at first with regurgitated food. By 16 weeks the young foxes no longer need their mother's milk. At one year old they are full grown, but they do not usually breed until the next year.

These maned wolf cubs are nearly full grown. Much of the grassland habitat of maned wolves has been lost and the wolves are now endangered.

Bush Dog

A group of bush dogs is patrolling the riverbank, looking for food. One dog spots a turtle on a rock, but the turtle slips into the water. The dog plunges its head into the water, trying to find the turtle. It lifts its head out, shakes, and then plunges in again. This time it comes up with the turtle in its teeth.

Unusual canids

Bush dogs live in rain forests and wet savanna areas in South America. They are unusual canids in many ways. They have a stocky body, short legs, and a stubby tail, similar to a terrier. But their head is more like an otter's, with a short muzzle and small, rounded ears. The bush dog is well-adapted for the life it leads. Long legs would be a nuisance in the heavy undergrowth of the rain forest. Its small ears and short muzzle look like an otter's because, like the otter, it is an excellent swimmer and spends a lot of its time in water. It also has webbed feet to help it swim and dive.

Bush dogs live close to water. They are excellent swimmers and divers, and hunt some of their prey in water.

Daytime hunters

Unlike the majority of canids, bush dogs are diurnal (active during the day). They are also the most sociable of the small canids. They live in groups of up to ten dogs, usually made up of members of the same family. At night they sleep together in a heap, hidden in a burrow or hollow tree trunk. In the morning they set off to patrol their territory. They run in single file, with the dominant female in front. The dogs make a whistle sound or yelp to keep in touch. As they patrol, they scent-mark their regular paths. Males spray urine to scent-mark by lifting their leg, like other canids. However, female bush dogs spray a tree or other landmark by reversing up it into a kind of handstand, and spraying in this position. Along their patrol route they keep a sharp lookout for possible prey.

Catching larger prey

Bush dogs most often hunt large rodents such as agoutis (fast-running relatives of guinea pigs). They also sometimes hunt in packs so they can catch prey much bigger than themselves, such as capybaras (large rodents), and ostrich-like birds called rheas. Capybaras often dive into water, but this does not help them to escape from a pack of bush dogs.

Young foxes fight among themselves for food, but bush dogs are more sociable and are happy to eat together.

Bringing up pups

Little is known about bush dog breeding. Females usually give birth to three or four pups about two months after mating. The young are dependent upon their mother's milk for about eight weeks, and by ten months they are fully grown.

Dingo

The fence is over 7 ft (2 m) high and topped with barbed wire. It runs 3,400 mi (5,500 km) from the south coast of Australia to halfway up the east coast, separating the southeast corner from the rest of the continent. It is the dog or dingo fence, built to keep dingoes away from southeast Australian sheep farms.

Close to dogs

Dingoes are wild dogs, closely related to wolves and domestic (pet) dogs. They are found in Australia, Southeast Asia, and in New Guinea. Dingoes are not native to Australia. They were introduced into the country thousands of years ago by humans. The oldest dingo fossil in Australia is about 3,500 years old, but dingoes are thought to have arrived much earlier than this. Dingoes are about 73 in. (185 cm) from head to tail. Most dingoes are a gingery or red color, with white markings on the feet and chest. They live in different habitats, from dry deserts to rain forests. Like most canids, they are nocturnal.

Mating and young

Dingoes sometimes live in pairs, but in some areas they live in groups. Like wolves, only the dominant pair mate and produce pups. Mating takes place during the Australian fall, and the pups are born nine weeks later. There are typically five or six pups in a litter. The pups feed on their mother's milk for two months, and by six months they are independent.

Pure dingoes, like these, are usually gingery colored, but to be certain they are pure-bred, the skull and teeth have to be measured and checked.

Dingoes are adaptable hunters and will eat whatever food they can catch. This dingo is chasing a monitor lizard through the water.

Adaptable feeders

The most important prey for dingoes are kangaroos, wallabies, and their relatives. Dingoes hunt wallabies alone or in pairs, but to catch larger prey, such as kangaroos, they hunt in packs. As with other canids, dingoes are adaptable feeders. In the central Australian desert, for instance, they live on lizards, rabbits, and rodents. They also kill and eat sheep.

Threatened by dogs

Dingoes have survived many years of being hunted by humans, but more recently they have become threatened by a less obvious danger. Dingoes and domestic dogs are very closely related, and in some areas they have bred together. If such cross-breeding continues, the dingo will cease to exist as a separate species.

Killing off devils

There is strong evidence to suggest that the arrival of dingoes in Australia led to the extinction of two marsupial carnivores on the Australian mainland— the thylacine (Tasmanian tiger) and the Tasmanian devil. As their names suggest, both these animals survived on the island of Tasmania, where there were no dingoes. However, the thylacine was heavily hunted by humans in the 19th century and is now extinct.

Dhole

Crashing sounds and the whistling calls of other dholes are coming from the forest at the edge of the clearing. But the dholes waiting in the long grass stay quiet and alert. With a final crash, a large chital stag comes bounding out of the trees. Leaping from their hiding places, the dholes rush in for the kill.

Asian dogs

Dholes (pronounced "doles") are Asian wild dogs. They are forest-dwellers, living in the steamy rain forests of India and the conifer forests of Siberia. Rain forest dholes have a thin coat of fur all year, but Siberian dholes grow a thicker coat in winter to help them survive the cold conditions.

Dholes are about the size of a collie dog, 51 to 53 in. (130 to 135 cm) long including their tail, which is about 18 in. (45 cm) long. They have a short muzzle and rounded ears.

More than most canids, dholes are meat-eaters. Their short muzzle gives them a powerful bite and their meat-slicing teeth (see page 4) are especially large and sharp.

Living in packs

Like wolves, dholes live in packs. An average pack has about eight adults, with more males than females, and as many cubs. Outside the breeding season, several packs may gather together in clans of 40 or more for a short time.

Once they have made a kill, dholes eat fast. They will defend a kill from other predators, even driving away tigers and bears.

It is not known whether only one pair in a pack mate, as in wolves. After mating a female dhole prepares a den and nine weeks later she gives birth to between two and ten pups. Other pack members help bring up the pups. One pack member may guard the den while the rest of the pack hunts. And once the pups start to eat solid food, pack members will regurgitate food for them.

Hunting strategies

A dhole pack hunts large prey such as chital deer, reindeer, mountain sheep, and wild boar. Because they often live in dense forest, dholes cannot hunt in the same way as wolves. One way they hunt is for some of the pack to drive prey toward a clearing where other pack members lie in wait. Another strategy is to move through the forest abreast in a line and attack any prey that they disturb.

The short muzzle of a dhole gives it an extremely powerful bite.

Disappearing dholes

There are fears that populations of dholes are dangerously low in many areas where they live. In India, tiger reserves often provide good habitat for dholes, but there seem to be far fewer dholes here than could be expected. In central Asia and other areas, the forests that the dholes live in are being cut down for timber or to make way for farming.

African Wild Dog

The impala has been running now for 2 mi (3 km), and it is tired, but the African wild dogs chasing it seem tireless. Every time the impala tries to break away, a dog heads it off. The impala stumbles, and the hunt is over in seconds. Two dogs attack the impala's sides and one leaps for its nose. The impala falls, and the dogs rip open its belly.

Painted dogs

African wild dogs are also called painted dogs, because their bodies are covered in patterns of black, white, gray, and yellow splotches. Each individual's pattern is as unique as a fingerprint. African wild dogs are about the size of an Alsatian. They are between 41 and 65 in. (105 and 164 cm) long, 12 to 17 in. (30 to 44 cm) of which is tail. They have short muzzles that give them a very powerful bite, and large, rounded ears.

African wild dogs are found only in Africa. They prefer to live in savanna or other open country. In the past they were found throughout Africa, but today they are restricted to protected areas such as national parks, and places where there are few people.

When wild dogs gather after resting, or being apart, they greet each other by rubbing muzzles and yelping excitedly.

Beginning a hunt

African wild dogs are crepuscular, which means that they are most active in the mornings and evenings. Like dholes, they eat large prey that they hunt in packs. When the pack meets up to hunt at dawn or in the early evening, they rub and lick each other in greeting. The older dogs decide which way the pack will go, and they set off at an easy trot. The pack stays together in a loose formation, all of them on the lookout for prey.

Catching prey

When the pack finds a group of prey animals such as impala or Thompson's gazelles, they will single out a weaker individual and give chase. Over short distances gazelles can outrun wild dogs, but the dogs are tireless, and keep up the chase until their prey begin to weaken. During the hunt the dogs keep in touch with soft hooting calls.

An experienced dog can bring down a gazelle or similar-sized prey alone, but usually several dogs will be involved. The most experienced hunter will often leap at the animal's head and clamp its jaws around its lip or nose.

African wild dogs most commonly hunt medium-sized grazers, such as gazelles and antelopes, but they sometimes can hunt prey up to the size of zebra and wildebeest.

A pack of wild dogs have run this young wildebeest to a standstill. Now one of the dogs grabs the wildebeest's sensitive nose and tries to pull it down.

Social dogs

African wild dogs are highly sociable. They eat, sleep, play, and hunt together. Like wolves and dholes, African wild dogs live in packs of between 2 and 30.

A pack is started when a group of sisters that have left their home pack meet up with a group of brothers (usually a larger group) that have left their home pack. One male and female establish themselves as the dominant pair, and the pack begins to live and hunt together.

Mating and young

Usually only the dominant pair in a pack will mate. The pair prepare a den (often the old burrow of a warthog or other animal) and about ten weeks after mating the female gives birth to her pups. African bush dogs have large litters. The average litter size is ten. As with other canids the pups spend three weeks or so in the den. During this time the pack hunts around the den area. Once the pups are four or five weeks old, pack members help to feed them with regurgitated meat.

Once the pups are about fifteen weeks old they follow the pack when they hunt. The pack now no longer returns to the den after hunting, but ranges over a much wider area. When the pack makes a kill, the youngsters are allowed to eat first. At thirteen to fourteen months old, African wild dogs are mature, but they stay with the pack to help with next year's pups. Females usually leave after about two years, but males stay on longer. Some males may stay with their home pack their whole life, but others leave after three years or so.

For two or three months while the pups are growing up, pack members hunt in the area of the den, so that they can bring food to the hungry youngsters.

Disappearing dogs

Experts think that there are fewer than 5,000 African wild dogs in the whole of Africa, and the species is seriously endangered. There are many reasons for this. But the main problem is that African wild dogs need huge amounts of space to live in, and the areas of habitat where they can roam freely are getting smaller and smaller. The population is split into small groups, each separated from the others. Where there are populations of 100 or more African wild dogs, the species should survive if they and their habitat are protected. But populations of 20 or fewer are unlikely to survive.

African wild dogs need a territory of least 150 sq mi (400 sq km). In areas where food is scarce each pack may need a territory of 770 sq mi (2,000 sq km).

Classification Chart

Scientists classify living things by comparing different kinds and deciding how closely related to each other they are. They then sort the millions of different living things into groups. Different species of living things that are closely related are put together in a larger group called a genus (plural genera). Similar genera are grouped into families, and similar families are grouped together in orders. Closely related orders are grouped into classes, classes are grouped into phyla, and phyla are put together in huge groups called kingdoms. Wolves and dogs make up the canid family (Canidae) within the order Carnivora (carnivores). Carnivores belong to the class Mammalia (mammals).

Canid genera

Genus	Number of species	Examples
Wolves and "true" dogs (Canis)	9	wolf, domestic dog, dingo, jackals, coyote, Ethiopian wolf
Gray foxes (Urocyon)	2	gray fox, island gray fox
Bat-eared foxes (Otocyon)	1	bat-eared fox
Foxes (Vulpes)	12	red fox, fennec fox, Arctic fox
Zorros (Dusicyon)	8	culpeo zorro, crab-eating zorro
African wild dogs (Lycaon)	1	African wild dog
Dholes (Cuon)	1	dhole
Maned wolves (Chrysocyon)	1	maned wolf
Bush dogs (Speothos)	1	bush dog
Raccoon dog (Nyctereutes)	1	raccoon dog
Small-eared dogs (Atelocynus)	1	small-eared dog

Where Wolves and Dogs Live

These maps show where some of the wolves and dogs in this book live.

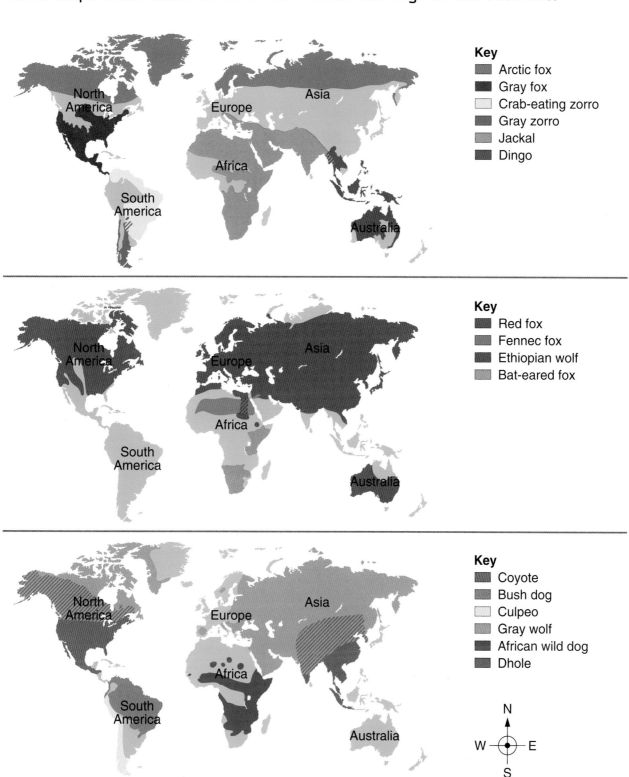

Key
- Arctic fox
- Gray fox
- Crab-eating zorro
- Gray zorro
- Jackal
- Dingo

Key
- Red fox
- Fennec fox
- Ethiopian wolf
- Bat-eared fox

Key
- Coyote
- Bush dog
- Culpeo
- Gray wolf
- African wild dog
- Dhole

Glossary

adapted way in which living things gradually change to fit in with their environment

breed to mate and produce young

breeding season some animals breed only at a certain time each year: their breeding season

canid family of mammals that includes dogs, wolves, and foxes

carnivore meat-eater

carrion dead and rotting meat

descendant the offspring of an animal: children, grandchildren, and so on

domesticated trained to live with people

dominant more powerful or important

endangered when an animal or plant species is in danger of dying out completely

evaporate when water turns from a liquid to a gas, it evaporates

extinct/extinction when a whole species of living things die out

family group or genera of living things that are closely related

fossil remains of an animal or plant that have been in the ground for many years and have become hard like rock

genus (plural genera) group of species of living things that are closely related

habitat place where an animal lives

hibernate to go into a deep sleep through the winter

home range area that an animal or group of animals lives

hybrid animal or plant produced by breeding together two different species

immunize give a medicine or injection to protect against disease

inbreeding when closely related animals breed together. Inbreeding can cause young to be weak or deformed.

insulator material that stops heat from passing through it

kit young fox

larva (plural larvae) the young stage in the life cycle of an insect

litter young born to a female in one birth

livestock farm animals, such as cattle

mammal hairy, warm-blooded animal that feeds its young on breast milk

marsupial mammal such as a kangaroo that has a pouch where its babies grow and develop after birth

mate when a male inserts sperm into a female animal to fertilize her eggs

nocturnal active at night

omnivore animal that eats both meat and plant food

pampas wide grasslands in South America

parasite creature that lives and feeds on or in another living creature, without giving any benefit in return

predator animal that hunts and eats other animals

prey animal that is hunted by a predator

regurgitate bring up food that has already been swallowed

rodent mammal with large, chisel-like front teeth, such as a rat or a squirrel

savanna grassland in Africa with scattered bushes and trees

scavenge eat dead meat or garbage

scent-marking marking a territory with urine or droppings

species group of animals that are similar and can breed together to produce young

territory area around an animal's home that it defends from other animals of the same species

tundra cold, bleak lands that are covered with snow for most of the year

vaccine a medicine that stimulates the body's defenses against a particular disease

vixen female fox

Further Reading

Eckart, Edana. *Gray Wolf.* Danbury, Conn.: Scholastic Library, 2003.

Gentle, Victor and Janet Perry. *African Wild Dogs.* Milwaukee: Gareth Stevens, 2002.

Gentle, Victor and Janet Perry. *Jackals.* Milwaukee: Gareth Stevens, 2002.

Markle, Sandra. *Predators.* New York: Scholastic, 2003.

Murdico, Suzanne J. *Coyote Attacks.* Danbury, Conn.: Scholastic Library, 2000.

Index